EXECUTIVE SUMMARY

Algeria is a multiparty republic whose president, the head of state, is elected by popular vote for a five-year term. The president has the constitutional authority to appoint and dismiss cabinet members and the prime minister, who is the head of government. Presidential term limits, which were eliminated in 2008, were reintroduced in a 2016 revision of the constitution and limit the president to two five-year terms. Voters re-elected President Abdelaziz Bouteflika, who has held office since 1999, in the 2014 presidential elections. Foreign observers characterized the elections as largely peaceful but noted low voter turnout and a high rate of ballot invalidity. The 2012 legislative elections did not result in significant changes to the composition of the government.

Civilian authorities generally maintained effective control over the security forces.

The three most significant continuing human rights problems were restrictions on the freedom of assembly and association, lack of judicial independence and impartiality, and limits on freedom of the press.

Other human rights concerns were the excessive use of force by police, including allegations of torture; limitations on the ability of citizens to choose their government; widespread corruption accompanied by reports of limited government transparency; and societal discrimination against persons with disabilities, persons with HIV/AIDS, and lesbian, gay, bisexual, transgender, and intersex (LGBTI) persons. Women faced violence and discrimination, and there was some reported child abuse. Additionally, the government maintained restrictions on worker rights.

The government did not take sufficient steps to investigate, prosecute, or punish public officials who committed violations. Impunity for police and security officials remained a problem, and the government rarely provided information on actions taken against officials accused of wrongdoing.

Abuses by terrorist groups remained a significant problem. Terrorist groups committed attacks against the security services and targeted military personnel in particular.

Section 1. Respect for the Integrity of the Person, Including Freedom from:

a. Arbitrary Deprivation of Life and other Unlawful or Politically Motivated Killings

There were no reports that the government or its agents committed arbitrary or unlawful killings. In 2015 the deaths of two individuals in detention raised public concern. In September 2015 several newspapers reported that Benchikh Aissa died in a Ghardaia prison. His lawyers said he suffered from depression, and prison officials refused to provide necessary health services. Afari Baaouchi died several weeks earlier in a Laghouat prison. Authorities arrested both detainees in July 2015 in the wake of the clashes between Mozabite Ibadi Muslims and Arab Sunni Maliki Muslims in Ghardaia. The Algerian League for the Defense of Human Rights (LADDH) called for an official investigation into the deaths, but no public information was available at year's end on whether the government conducted investigations.

Some terrorist groups remained active in the country, including al-Qaida in the Islamic Maghreb and a Da'esh affiliate, Jund al-Khilafah, and attacked security services personnel. On April 15, terrorists killed four soldiers in Constantine Province. On August 6, an improvised explosive device killed four civilians in Khenchela Province. Da'esh (also known as the Islamic State of Iraq and the Levant) took credit for the October 28 killing of a police officer in Constantine. Terrorists reportedly killed two police officers and a civilian in a November 13 attack in Ain Defla.

b. Disappearance

There were no reports of politically motivated disappearances.

The government stated it was in discussion with the UN Human Rights Council Working Group on Enforced or Involuntary Disappearances regarding a visit to the country. The government regarded this as the next step to addressing cases of enforced or involuntary disappearances from the 1990s that the working group submitted to it in 2014.

Government officials declared there were 84 reported cases of child kidnapping in 2015 and 28 in the first half of 2016. Figures on total ransom payments were unavailable, since the government maintained a strict no-concessions policy with regard to individuals or groups holding its citizens hostage.

c. Torture and Other Cruel, Inhuman, or Degrading Treatment or Punishment

The law prohibits torture, but nongovernmental organizations (NGOs) and local human rights activists alleged that government officials sometimes employed torture and abusive treatment to obtain confessions. The government denied these charges. Government agents face prison sentences of between 10 and 20 years for committing such acts, and there were two convictions during the year. There were no other reported cases of prosecution of civil or military security service officials for torture or abusive treatment. Local and international NGOs asserted that impunity was a problem.

On May 12, the UN Human Rights Committee found the country to be in violation of article seven of the International Covenant on Civil and Political Rights, which prohibits torture and cruel, inhuman, or degrading treatment or punishment. The decision was based on the government's failure to contest allegations made in the case of financial consultant Chani Medjoub, who was initially arrested in 2009 in connection with a corruption case and who alleged that members of the judicial police of the Intelligence and Security Department (DRS) tortured him.

On May 25, two police officers were convicted and sentenced to seven and 15 years in prison, respectively, following their May 2015 arrests for raping a woman during her detention in a police station.

In September, LADDH called for an investigation into reports that male police officers in Ain Benian, west of Algiers, forced a detained 29-year-old woman with developmental disabilities to undress in front of them in the local police station. The woman's family reportedly filed a complaint with the local tribunal, but additional information was unavailable as of September.

The Surete Nationale (DGSN) stated that it did not receive any reports of abuse or misconduct from the public during the year. Information from the National Gendarmerie was not available.

Prison and Detention Center Conditions

Prison and detention center conditions generally met international standards.

A 2013 presidential decree dissolved the Central Bureau of the Judicial Police under the DRS, removing its authority to detain individuals and hold them in separate detention facilities. A 2014 presidential decree, however, reinstated this authority and permitted the DRS to manage prison facilities. A January 20 presidential decree dissolved the DRS and reorganized the intelligence services. The July 2015 amendment of the penal code prohibits police officers from detaining suspects in any facilities not designated for that purpose and declared to the local prosecutor, who has the right to visit such facilities at any time.

Physical Conditions: According to statistics provided in August, the Ministry of Justice's General Directorate for Prison Administration and Resettlement (DGAPR) had responsibility for approximately 60,000 prisoners. Convicted terrorists had the same rights as other inmates but were held in prisons of varying degrees of security, determined by whether authorities considered the prisoners highly dangerous or of high, intermediate, or low risk.

The government used specific facilities for prisoners age 27 and younger. With support from the British, Canadian, and French governments, the DGAPR modernized its inmate classification system and maintained different categories of prisons that separated prisoners among facilities according to the general lengths of their sentences. Several detention facilities reportedly operated at 200 to 300 percent of capacity. Some observers, including government-appointed human rights officials, attributed overcrowding in pretrial detention facilities to "excessive use" of pretrial detention.

Authorities generally transferred pretrial detainees, after presenting them before the prosecutor, to prisons and did not hold them in separate detention facilities. In some prisons pretrial detainees were held in cellblocks separate from those that housed the general prison population.

Administration: No ombudsman existed to serve on behalf of prisoners or detainees. Prisoners may submit uncensored complaints to penitentiary administration, doctors, and their judge. It was unclear how frequently prison authorities collected the complaints or requests. Authorities permitted family members to visit prisoners in standard facilities weekly and to provide detainees with food and clothing, although the common practice of holding inmates in prisons very far from their families discouraged visits. In the majority of the prisons, nonfunctional telephones further exacerbated the difficulty for detainees to maintain regular contact with family.

Independent Monitoring: The government allowed the International Committee of the Red Cross (ICRC) and local human rights observers to visit regular prisons and detention centers. ICRC staff visited prisons, police and gendarme stations under the jurisdiction of the Ministry of Justice, and an administrative detention center operated by the Ministry of Interior. By September the ICRC had visited 32 detention facilities, representing approximately one-third of the total prison population. Delegates paid special attention to vulnerable detainees, including foreigners, women, minors, persons in solitary confinement, and individuals held for security reasons by police and gendarmes. The ICRC provided the government confidential feedback, when applicable, to help authorities improve detainee treatment and living conditions, reinforce respect for judicial protections, and expand access to health care. During the year the ICRC hosted training sessions on human rights--as they relate to arrest, detention, and interrogation procedures--for judicial police from the DGSN and National Gendarmerie and judges.

Improvements: Authorities improved prison conditions to meet international standards. The Ministry of Justice's Directorate of Penal Affairs and Pardons announced that since 2010, the government opened 31 new detention centers. Of the new facilities, 10 were minimum-security centers that held prisoners in cells and permitted them to work. Intelligent camera systems were installed in some pretrial detention facilities to allow the DGSN to monitor conditions of detention.

d. Arbitrary Arrest or Detention

Overuse of pretrial detention remained a problem. Security forces routinely detained individuals who conducted activities against the order of the state such as protesting, striking, or rioting. Arrested individuals reported that authorities held them for four to eight hours before releasing them without charges.

Role of the Police and Security Apparatus

The 130,000-member National Gendarmerie, which performs police functions outside of urban areas under the auspices of the Ministry of National Defense, and the approximately 210,000-member DGSN or national police, organized under the Ministry of Interior, share general responsibility for maintaining law and order. A January 20 presidential decree dissolved the DRS, which had been subordinate to the Ministry of National Defense. It was replaced by three intelligence directorates reporting to a presidential national security counselor and performing functions related specifically to internal, external, and technical security.

Impunity remained a problem. The law provides mechanisms to investigate abuses and corruption, but the government did not always provide public information on disciplinary or legal action against police, military, or other security force personnel. The DGSN conducted a two-week training session for police officers specifically focusing on human rights practices in September and another two-day training session in November.

Arrest Procedures and Treatment of Detainees

According to the law, police must obtain a summons from the Prosecutor's Office to require a suspect to appear in a police station for preliminary questioning. With this summons police may hold a suspect for no more than 48 hours. Authorities also use summonses to notify and require the accused and the victim to attend a court proceeding or hearing. Police may make arrests without a warrant if they witness the offense. Public lawyers reported that authorities usually carried out procedures for warrants and summonses properly.

If authorities require time beyond the authorized 48-hour period for gathering additional evidence, they may extend a suspect's authorized time in police detention with the prosecutor's authorization in the following cases: once, if charges pertain to an attack on data processing systems; twice, if charges relate to state security; three times, for charges concerning drug trafficking, organized and transnational crime, money laundering, and other currency-related crimes; and five times (for a maximum of 12 days), for charges related to terrorism and other subversive activities. The law stipulates that detainees should immediately be able to contact a family member and receive a visit, or to contact an attorney. The 2015 report of the National Consultative Commission for the Promotion and Protection of Human Rights (CNCPPDH), a governmental human rights commission, criticized this provision for forcing detainees to choose between contacting their families and consulting an attorney.

The law provides detainees the right to see an attorney for 30 minutes if the time in detention has been extended beyond the initial 48-hour period. In these cases authorities permit the arrested person to contact a lawyer after half the extended time has expired. Authorities may use in court confessions and statements garnered during the period prior to access to an attorney--which a prosecutor's application to a judge may extend. The court appearance of suspects in terrorism cases is public. At the end of the period of detention, the detainee has the right to request a medical examination by a physician of choice within the jurisdiction of the court. Otherwise, the judicial police appoint a doctor. Authorities enter the certificate of the medical examination into the detainee's file.

In non-felony cases and in cases of individuals held on charges of terrorism and other subversive activities that exceed a 12-day period plus any authorized extension, the law calls for the release of suspects on provisional liberty, referred to as "judicial control," while awaiting trial. Under provisional liberty status, authorities subjected suspects to requirements such as reporting periodically to the police station in their district, stopping professional activities related to the alleged offense committed, surrendering all travel documents required to leave the country, and, in some terrorism-related cases, residing at an agreed-upon address. The law provides that foreigners may be required to furnish bail as a condition of release on provisional liberty status.

Judges rarely refused prosecutorial requests to extend pretrial detention, which by law may be appealed. Should the detention be overturned, the defendant has the right to request compensation. Most detainees had prompt access to a lawyer of their choice as accorded by law, and the government provided legal counsel to indigent detainees. There were reports that authorities held some detainees without access to their lawyers and reportedly abused them physically and mentally.

Various press outlets reported that in October 2015 National Gendarmerie officers told a Cameroonian female migrant, who claimed a group of Algerian men assaulted and raped her, that they could not file charges because she was an illegal migrant. The victim reported that several hospitals refused to provide her treatment and to issue her a certificate documenting her sexual assault. After social media and local civil society organizations mobilized over the issue, authorities accepted her complaint and arrested two of the eight alleged actors. As of September the status of the investigation was not known.

Arbitrary Arrest: Although the law prohibits arbitrary arrest and detention, authorities sometimes used vaguely worded provisions, such as "inciting an unarmed gathering" and "insulting a government body," to arrest and detain individuals considered to be disturbing public order or criticizing the government. Amnesty International (AI) and other human rights organizations criticized the law prohibiting unauthorized gatherings and called for its amendment to require only notification as opposed to application for authorization. These observers, among others, pointed to the law as a significant source of arbitrary arrests intended to suppress activist speech. Police arrested protesters in Algiers and elsewhere in the country throughout the year for violating the law against unregistered public gatherings.

On July 13, attorney and human rights activist Salah Debouz and six other activists were arrested at a cafe in Ghardaia and detained for eight hours for holding an unlawful gathering. The activists had been meeting near the local courthouse to discuss the case of one of Debouz's clients. Debouz had also been arrested on February 6 during a meeting with labor union activists and subsequently released the same day.

Authorities arrested Youcef Ouled Dada in March 2014 for "harming a national institution" and "insulting a government body" when he posted a video on Facebook that captured three police officers engaged in looting during riots in the city of Ghardaia. In September 2014 a Ghardaia court reaffirmed the two-year prison term and DZD 100,000 ($916) fine it imposed in June 2014 on Dada. He was released March 27 after two years in prison.

<u>Pretrial Detention</u>: Prolonged pretrial detention remained a serious problem. Nongovernmental observers believed pretrial detainees comprised a significant portion of the total detainee and prisoner population but admitted they did not have specific statistics. The Ministry of Justice said that as of September, the proportion of detainees in preventive detention was 13.85 percent of the total detainee and prisoner population, compared with 15.02 percent during the same period in 2015, and that the proportion in police custody was 5.66 percent. Ministry statistics did not include prisoners whose cases were pending appeal. July 2015 changes to the penal code limit the grounds for pretrial detention and stipulate that before it can be imposed, a judge must assess the gravity of a crime and whether the accused is a threat to society or a flight risk.

AI alleged that authorities sometimes detained individuals on security-related charges for longer than the 12-day prescribed period.

Authorities held KBC TV journalists Mehdi Benaissa and Ryad Hartouf and Ministry of Culture official Nora Nedjai in pretrial detention for 26 days. They were arrested on June 22 in connection with the alleged unauthorized production of satirical television programs that were broadcast in July. All three received suspended prison sentences and were released July 18.

Police arrested Nacer Eddine Hadjadj, former mayor of Beriane municipality and member of the Rally for Culture and Democracy party, in July 2015. Press reports indicated authorities detained Hadjadj for questioning regarding the violent events that took place in Ghardaia, but the government did not confirm this. In August 2015 Hadjadj's lawyer, Salah Debouz, denounced the government for not notifying him of his client's hearing for provisional liberty. The judge rejected his request for provisional liberty, and he remained in pretrial detention as of September.

The government implemented changes adopted in 2015 to the criminal procedure code that prohibit the use of pretrial detention for crimes with maximum punishments of less than three years imprisonment. The revised law, however, exempts infractions that resulted in deaths and persons considered a "threat to public order." In these cases the revised law limits the use of pretrial detention to one month, nonrenewable. The government also amended the criminal procedure code to state that in all other criminal cases, pretrial detention may not exceed four months. Representatives of the CNCPPDH said that the penal code amendments had succeeded in reducing the use of pretrial detention in 2016 but did not maintain their own statistics demonstrating a decrease from the previous year.

Judges rarely refused prosecutorial requests to extend pretrial detention, which by law may be appealed. Should the detention be overturned, the defendant has the right to request compensation. Most detainees had prompt access to a lawyer of their choice as accorded by law, and the government provided legal counsel to indigent detainees. There were reports that authorities held some detainees without access to their lawyers and reportedly abused them physically and mentally.

<u>Detainee's Ability to Challenge Lawfulness of Detention before a Court</u>: The Code of Criminal Procedure grants pre-trial detainees the right to appeal a court's order of pre-trial detention. The appeal must be filed within three days. A person released from custody following a dismissal or acquittal may apply to a civil commission to seek compensation from the government for "particular and particularly severe" harm caused by pre-trial detention. The person must submit an application for compensation within six months of the dismissal or acquittal.

e. Denial of Fair Public Trial

While the constitution provides for the separation of powers between the executive and judicial branches of government, the executive branch's broad statutory authorities limited judicial independence. The constitution grants the president authority to appoint all prosecutors and judges. These presidential appointments are not subject to legislative oversight but are reviewed by the High Judicial Council, which consists of the president, minister of justice, chief prosecutor of the Supreme Court, 10 judges, and six individuals outside the judiciary chosen by the president. The president serves as the president of the High Judicial Council, which is also responsible for the appointment, transfer, promotion, and discipline of judges. The judiciary was not impartial and was often subject to influence and corruption.

Trial Procedures

The constitution provides for the right to a fair trial, but authorities did not always respect legal provisions that protect defendants' rights. The law presumes defendants are innocent and have the right to be present and to consult with an attorney provided at public expense if necessary. Most trials are public, except when the judge determines the proceedings to be a threat to public order or "morals." The July 2015 amendment of the penal code guarantees defendants the right to free interpretation as necessary. Defendants have the right to be present during their trial but may be tried in absentia if they do respond to a summons ordering their appearance.

Defendants may confront or question witnesses against them or present witnesses and evidence on their behalf. There were a few reports that courts occasionally denied defendants and their attorneys' access to government-held evidence. Defendants have the right not to be compelled to testify or confess guilt, and they have the right to appeal. The testimony of men and women has equal weight under the law.

Political Prisoners and Detainees

International and local observers alleged that authorities used antiterrorism laws and restrictive laws on freedom of expression and public assembly to detain political activists and outspoken critics of the government.

In March 2015 the National Coordination of Families of Political Prisoners called for the release of 160 persons who had remained incarcerated since the 1990s. In April 2015 Prime Minister Abdelmalek Sellal stated the government held no political prisoners. He declared that courts convicted the detainees in question of violent crimes, making them ineligible for government pardons under the National Charter for Peace and Reconciliation. The government permitted the ICRC to visit detainees held for "security reasons."

On March 7, a Tamanrasset court convicted Committee for the Defense of the Rights of Unemployed Workers activist Abdelali Ghellam to a year in prison following his December 2015 arrest on charges of taking part in an unauthorized gathering and obstructing traffic. AI reported that seven other men were also arrested in connection with the same protest and received one-year sentences and DZD 50,000 ($458) fines.

Civil Judicial Procedures and Remedies

The judiciary was neither independent nor impartial in civil matters and lacked independence in some human rights cases. Family connections and status of the parties involved influenced decisions. Individuals may bring lawsuits, and administrative processes related to amnesty may provide damages to the victims or their families for human rights violations and compensation for alleged wrongs. Individuals may appeal adverse decisions to international human rights bodies, but their decisions would not have the force of law.

f. Arbitrary or Unlawful Interference with Privacy, Family, Home, or Correspondence

The constitution provides for the protection of a person's "honor" and private life, including the privacy of home, communication, and correspondence, although government authorities infringed on citizens' privacy rights. According to human rights activists, citizens widely believed the government conducted frequent electronic surveillance of a range of citizens, including political opponents, journalists, human rights groups, and suspected terrorists. Security officials reportedly searched homes without a warrant. Security forces conducted unannounced home visits.

The government established a new anticybercrime agency charged with coordinating anticybercrime efforts and engaging in preventive surveillance of electronic communications in the interests of national security. Falling under the purview of the Ministry of Justice, the agency has exclusive authority for monitoring all electronic surveillance activities, but the decree did not provide details regarding the limits of surveillance authority or corresponding protections for persons subject to surveillance. The Ministry of Justice said the agency was subject to all existing judicial controls that apply to law enforcement agencies.

Section 2. Respect for Civil Liberties, Including:

a. Freedom of Speech and Press

The constitution provides for freedom of speech and press, and independent media outlets criticized government officials and policies, but the government restricted these rights. The government's techniques included harassment of some critics; arbitrary enforcement of vaguely worded laws; informal pressure on publishers, editors, advertisers, and journalists; and control of a significant proportion of the country's advertising money and printing capabilities. Some media figures alleged the government used its control over most printing houses and large amounts of public sector advertising preferentially, and that the lack of clear regulations over these practices permitted it to exert undue influence on press outlets.

<u>Freedom of Speech and Expression</u>: Individuals were limited in their ability to criticize the government publicly without reprisal. Authorities arrested and detained citizens for doing so, and citizens practiced self-restraint in expressing public criticism. The law criminalizing speech about the conduct of the security forces during the internal conflict of the 1990s remained in force, although there were no cases of arrest or prosecution under the law during the year. The law provides for up to three years' imprisonment for tracts, bulletins, or flyers that "may harm the national interest" or up to one year for defaming or insulting the president, parliament, army, or state institutions. Government officials monitored political meetings. Authorities used laws against slander of public officials to restrict public discussion.

On August 3, the government published a law passed by parliament that broadens laws on defamation to cover the conduct of retired military officers. The law specifies that retired officers who engage in a "dereliction of duty that harms the honor and respect due to state institutions constitutes an outrage and defamation" and can result in legal action under applicable laws. The law further prohibits speech that damages "the authority and the public image of the military institution."

In March a court in Tlemcen issued human rights activist Zoulikha Belarbi a DZD 100,000 ($916) fine for posting a photograph on Facebook that was deemed insulting to President Bouteflika. The offending post showed a retouched image of the president and other political figures that made them look like characters from a Turkish television show, according to Human Rights Watch (HRW).

<u>Press and Media Freedoms</u>: The National Agency for Publishing and Advertising (ANEP) controls public advertising for print media. According to the NGO Reporters without Borders, private advertising existed but frequently came from businesses with close links to the ruling political party. In September 2015 ANEP stated it represented only half of the total advertising market, while nongovernmental sources assessed the majority of daily newspapers depended on

ANEP-authorized advertising to finance their operations. Minister of Communication Hamid Grine stated in February that ANEP's budget had been cut by 50 percent. The government's lack of transparency over its use of state-funded advertising permitted it to exert undue influence over print media.

Activists and journalists criticized the government for criminally prosecuting two KBC TV journalists, Mehdi Benaissa and Ryad Hartouf, for allegedly making false statements in their applications for filming permits and their alleged unauthorized use of a television studio. The studio had previously belonged to Al-Atlas TV, which authorities shut down in 2014. In addition to the arrests of Benaissa and Hartouf, authorities shut down two of KBC's political satire programs, which were filmed in the studio in question. Benaissa and Hartouf's suspended sentences were announced on July 18, shortly after a court on July 13 canceled the sale of KBC's parent company, El Khabar Group, to a subsidiary of a company owned by businessman Issad Rebrab, who has been critical of the government. The Ministry of Communication, which had sued to cancel the transaction, said the ruling was based on the law's prohibition on one person owning multiple news outlets.

In October 2015 Algiers police raided the headquarters of El-Watan El-Djazairya, a private, foreign-based television station broadcasting in the country, and closed down the station upon orders of the Algiers mayor. Minister of Communication Grine accused the television station of "harming a state symbol" during an interview it transmitted on October 3, 2015, with the former emir of the Islamic Salvation Army, Madani Mezrag. During the interview Mezrag indirectly threatened President Bouteflika after the president affirmed the government would not let Mezrag form a political party due to his connection to terrorist activities. In September, Djaafar Chelli, the former owner of El Watan El-Djazairya, received a DZD 10 million ($91,575) fine for broadcasting the interview with Mezrag.

Many civil society organizations, government opponents, and political parties, including legal Islamist parties, had access to independent print and broadcast media and used them to express their views. Opposition parties also disseminated information via the internet and published communiques but stated they did not have access to the national television and radio. Journalists from independent print and broadcast media expressed frustration over the near impossibility of receiving information from public officials. With the exception of several daily newspapers, the majority of print media outlets relied on the government for physical printing materials and operations.

In January a court reclassified a charge against journalist and LADDH board member Hassan Bouras, resulting in his release from El Bayadh prison after three months in custody. Prosecutors had charged Bouras in October 2015 with insulting a government body and inciting armed conflict against the state. As of November charges against Bouras had not been dropped, according to his lawyer. Separately, in November an El Bayadh court indicted Bouras for producing a video alleging that certain police officials and judges were involved in corruption. The court on November 28 convicted Bouras of complicity in offending a judicial officer, law enforcement officers, and a public body and of unlawfully practicing a profession regulated by law, sentencing him to one year in prison plus fines. Bouras's appeal remained pending at year's end.

Organizations wishing to initiate regular publications must obtain authorization from the government. The law requires the director of the publication to hold Algerian citizenship. The law additionally prohibits local periodicals from receiving direct or indirect material support from foreign sources. The CNCPPDH noted in its 2014 annual report that lack of a law controlling advertising was the largest hurdle to improving transparency of the distribution of public advertising (see also section 5). In May CNCPPDH president Farouk Ksentini said that depriving certain newspapers of public advertising revenue was "contrary to democracy and a violation of the constitution."

In September the Ministry of Communication stated there were 332 accredited written publications, which included 149 daily newspapers, 47 weekly and 75 monthly magazines, and other specialized publications. Of the daily printed publications, the ministry stated six were state-operated.

The ministry's Media Directorate is responsible for issuing and renewing accreditations to foreign media outlets operating in the country. Although this accreditation is required to operate legally, the vast majority of foreign media were not accredited. While the government tolerated their operations in the past, Minister Grine stated in April the number of private satellite channels that would receive frequencies would be limited to 13. He said in September that foreign-based unaccredited television outlets would be shut down. As of year's end, however, the government had not shut down any such outlets. On June 20, the government instated the Audiovisual Regulatory Authority (ARAV), a nine-member body that regulates television and radio. In August ARAV published regulations that require the shareholders and managers of any radio or television channel to be Algerian citizens and prohibits them from broadcasting content that offends "values anchored in Algerian society."

The ministry also issues and renews accreditation of foreign correspondents reporting in the country. According to the ministry, 13 accredited foreign press agencies reported during the year. In addition to five private domestic television channels, 12 foreign broadcasting channels and two foreign radio stations operated throughout the year.

The law mandates that online news outlets must inform the government of their activities but does not require them to request authorization to operate.

Violence and Harassment: News sources critical of the government reported instances of government harassment and intimidation due to their reporting. Government officials arrested and temporarily detained journalists.

On June 27, police arrested Mohamed Tamalt, a freelance journalist and blogger based in the United Kingdom. He was charged with insulting President Bouteflika on Facebook and sentenced to two years in prison and a DZD 200,000 ($1,832) fine. On December 11, Tamalt died following a prolonged hunger strike protesting his arrest and continued imprisonment.

On June 21, police officers encircled the new headquarters of the *El Watan* daily newspaper and ordered its staff to vacate the building. Local officials said the building did not conform to the construction permits granted by the government. As of September *El Watan* had not been permitted to take occupancy of the building.

Censorship or Content Restrictions: Some major news outlets faced direct and indirect retaliation for criticism of the government.

Some observers viewed the July conviction of two KBC TV journalists and the cancelation of the sale of KBC's parent company, El Khabar Group, as motivated by the political views expressed in KBC's programming and by the owner of the company that attempted to purchase El Khabar Group.

On May 3, Minister Grine called on private companies to cease advertising in three unnamed newspapers, widely assumed to be the *El Khabar*, *El Watan*, and *Liberte* newspapers, viewed as critical of the government. In an interview published online that day, the director general of *El Khabar* said Minister Grine's opposition to *El Khabar* was based on the fact that it "does not follow the editorial line that he wishes."

In a May 23 speech calling for unaccredited foreign satellite channels to be shut down, Prime Minister Sellal criticized channels that "use misleading advertising, violate private life, strike a blow to the dignity of persons, spread disinformation, and worse still, attack the cohesion of Algerian society through calls for hatred, regionalism, and chaos."

Libel/Slander Laws: NGOs and observers criticized the law on defamation as vaguely drafted and the definitions therein as failing to comport with internationally recognized norms. The law defines defamation as "any allegation or imputation of a fact offending the honor or consideration of a person, or of the body to which the fact is imputed." The law does not require that the fact alleged or imputed be false or that the statement be made with malicious intent to damage another individual's reputation. Defamation is not a crime but carries a fine ranging from DZD 100,000 to DZD 500,000 ($916 to $4,579). The Ministry of Justice did not provide information on the percentage of defamation claims that originated from private citizens, as opposed to government officials.

The law criminalizes statements denigrating Islam or insulting the Prophet Mohammed or "messengers of God." On June 14, the National Gendarmerie published a press release saying it had "dismantled an international criminal network of blasphemers and anti-Muslim proselytizers on the internet." News reports appeared to reference the case when they reported the arrests of Rachid Fodil and one or two other men in M'Sila Province, but the status of charges against them was unclear as of September. On July 31, police in Setif arrested Slimane Bouhafs, a Christian convert, for posting statements on his Facebook page questioning the morals of the Prophet Mohammed. A court tried and convicted Bouhafs the same day and sentenced him on August 7 to five years in prison, plus a DZD 100,000 ($916) fine. On September 6, his sentence was reduced to three years in prison.

Mohamed Chergui, a journalist for the *El-Djoumhouria* newspaper, was sentenced to three years in prison and a DZD 200,000 ($1,832) fine in February 2015 for a column he wrote in 2014 that was deemed offensive to the Prophet Mohammed and Islam. In April an appeals court in Oran overturned his conviction and ordered his release.

Internet Freedom

The government impeded access to the internet and monitored certain e-mail and social media sites. On June 18, state-run media reported the government planned to block access to social media sites, including Facebook and Twitter, on June 19-23 during nationwide high school exams. The decision was in response to previous leaks of exam results, which were posted on social media earlier in the month. On June 19-20, internet users reported that access to not only social media, but nearly all websites, was blocked. While internet service returned on June 20, access to social media was not fully restored until June 24.

In January police arrested an activist for the unemployed, Belkacem Khencha, and in May he was sentenced to six months in prison for posting a video on Facebook criticizing the judicial system's handling of arrests of fellow activists.

In a July statement, the human rights organization Collective of Families of the Disappeared said the government had blocked Radio of the Voiceless, the online radio station it launched in June, making it inaccessible to the public.

Internet users regularly exercised their right to free expression and association online, including through online forums, social media, and e-mail. Activists reported that some postings on social media could result in arrest and questioning; observers widely understood that the intelligence services closely monitored the activities of political and human rights activists on social media sites, including Facebook.

The law on cybercrime establishes procedures for using electronic data in prosecutions and outlines the responsibilities of service providers to cooperate with authorities. Under the law the government may conduct electronic surveillance operations to prevent offenses amounting to terrorist or subversive acts and infractions against state security, pursuant to written authorization from a competent judicial authority.

By law internet service providers face criminal penalties for the material and websites they host, especially if subject matters are "incompatible with morality or public opinion." The Ministries of Justice, Interior, and Post, Information Technology, and Communication have oversight responsibilities. The law provides sentences of six months to five years in prison and fines between DZD 50,000 and DZD 500,000 ($458 and $4,579) for users who do not comply with the law, including the obligation to cooperate with law enforcement authorities against cybercrime.

In September the government estimated there were 18,583,427 internet users in the country in 2015. According to the International Telecommunication Union, 38.2 percent of the population used the internet in 2015.

Academic Freedom and Cultural Events

Academic seminars and colloquia occurred with limited governmental interference. The Ministry of Culture reviewed the content of films before they could be shown, as well as books before publication or importation. The Ministry of Religious Affairs did the same for religious publications.

b. Freedom of Peaceful Assembly and Association

Although the constitution provides for freedom of assembly and association, the government severely restricted the exercise of these rights.

Freedom of Assembly

The constitution provides for the right of assembly, but the government continued to curtail this right. A ban on demonstrations in Algiers remained in effect. Authorities utilized the ban to prohibit assembly within the city limits. Nationwide, the government required citizens and organizations to obtain permits from the government-appointed local governor before holding public meetings or demonstrations. The government restricted licenses to political parties, NGOs, and other groups to hold indoor rallies or delayed permission until the eve of the event, thereby impeding publicity and outreach efforts by organizers. Nonetheless, in many cases authorities allowed unauthorized protests to proceed while negotiations continued regarding the protesters' demands or when government attempts to disperse protests potentially risked igniting violence.

On March 21, media outlets reported that police shoved and kicked protesters gathered in front of the Central Post Office in Algiers to demand permanent positions for teachers working on fixed-term contracts. Two women sought hospital treatment for injuries, according to HRW. On April 4, police stopped hundreds of protesting teachers in Boudouaou, preventing them from completing the final leg of a 140-mile march from Bejaia to Algiers. Protesters remained camped in Boudouaou until April 18, at which point police grabbed and shoved some protesters and loaded them onto buses.

Hotels in Algiers and other major cities continued their historic practice of refusing to sign rental contracts for meeting spaces with political parties, NGOs, and civil associations without a copy of a written authorization from the Ministry of Interior for the proposed gathering.

Throughout the year police dispersed unauthorized gatherings or prevented marching groups of protesters from demonstrating. Police typically dispersed protesters shortly after a protest began and arrested and detained organizers for a few hours. HRW, AI, and other NGOs criticized the government's use of the law to restrict peaceful assembly.

In July police reportedly arrested more than 100 communal guards arriving in Algiers en route to a planned demonstration outside of parliament. In June authorities arrested several Movement for the Autonomy of Kabylie (MAK) activists who were preparing to hold an unauthorized meeting in Larbaa Nath Irathen to mark the 15th anniversary of a Berber-led protest in Algiers. Clashes ensued when area residents gathered in the town center to demand the activists' release, resulting in injuries to police and some demonstrators, according to press reports. In February MAK president Bouaziz Ait Chebib stated to the *El Watan* newspaper that approximately 100 MAK activists had been briefly arrested in Tizi Ouzou to prevent their attendance at the MAK's national assembly.

Freedom of Association

The constitution provides for the right of association, but the government severely restricted this right.

The law's extensive requirements and uneven enforcement served as major impediments to the development of civil society. The law grants the government wide-ranging oversight of and influence in the day-to-day activities of civil society organizations. It requires national-level civil organizations to apply to the Ministry of Interior for permission to operate. Once registered, organizations must inform the government of their activities, funding sources, and personnel, including notification of personnel changes. The law imposes an additional requirement that associations obtain government preapproval before accepting foreign funds. If organizations fail to provide required information to the government or attempt to operate with or accept foreign funds without authorization, they are subject to fines between DZD 2,000 and DZD 5,000 ($18 and $46) and up to six months' imprisonment. The law prohibits formation of a political party with a religious platform, but observers stated they knew some political parties were Islamist.

According to the law, associations that apply for accreditation as required by law are entitled to receive a response regarding their application within two months for national organizations, 45 days for interregional-level associations, 40 days for province-level associations, and 30 days for communal organizations. While the Ministry of Interior oversees the accreditation process for most associations, the president of a local assembly approves applications for communal associations.

The Ministry of Interior may deny a license to or dissolve any group regarded as a threat to the government's authority or to public order, and on several occasions failed to grant in an expeditious fashion official recognition to NGOs, associations, religious groups, and political parties. According to the Ministry of Interior, organizations receive a deposit slip after submitting their application for accreditation, and after the time periods listed above, this slip is legally sufficient for them to begin operating, to open a bank account, and to rent office or event space. The law does not explicitly include this provision, however. If the application is approved, the Ministry of Interior issues a final accreditation document.

Many organizations reported that they never received a deposit slip and that even with the deposit slip it was difficult to conduct necessary administrative tasks without the formal accreditation. Other organizations reported that they never received any written response to their application request. The ministry maintained that organizations refused accreditation or that did not receive a response within the specified time periods were able to submit an appeal to the State Council, the administrative court responsible for cases involving the government.

During the year the Youth Action Movement, a civil society youth organization, was again unsuccessful in renewing its license despite submitting all documentation required by the Ministry of Interior. The ministry also did not renew the accreditations of the NGOs SOS Disparu (Missing) and LADDH, which submitted their renewal applications in 2013. According to members of the National Association for the Fight Against Corruption, the Ministry of Interior refused to approve the organization's request for accreditation, stating that the application did comply with the law on associations but did not provide any further information. The organization first submitted its application for accreditation in 2012.

The government issued licenses and subsidies to domestic associations, especially youth, medical, and neighborhood associations. According to the Ministry of Interior, there were 108,940 local and 1,293 national associations registered. A 2015 study conducted by several prominent domestic civil society organizations found, however, that nearly two-thirds of the approximately 93,000 associations registered with the government when the law on associations went into force in 2012 were either inactive or no longer operating. Unlicensed NGOs did not receive government assistance, and citizens at times hesitated to associate with these organizations.

c. Freedom of Religion

See the Department of State's *International Religious Freedom Report* at www.state.gov/religiousfreedomreport/.

d. Freedom of Movement, Internally Displaced Persons, Protection of Refugees, and Stateless Persons

The constitution provides for freedom of internal movement, foreign travel, emigration, and repatriation, but the government restricted the exercise of this right.

The government generally cooperated with the UN High Commissioner for Refugees (UNHCR) and other humanitarian organizations in providing protection and assistance to refugees, asylum seekers, and other persons of concern.

In-country Movement: The government maintained restrictions for security reasons on travel into the southern locales of El-Oued and Illizi, near hydrocarbon industry installations and the Libyan border, respectively. Citing the threat of terrorism, the government also prevented overland tourist travel between the southern cities of Tamanrasset, Djanet, and Illizi. Newspapers reported that the government restricted foreign tourists from traveling through trails in Tassili and Hoggar, as well as certain areas in and around Tamanrasset, due to security concerns. Civil society organizations reported that the authorities prevented sub-Saharan migrants in the areas around Tamanrasset from traveling north toward coastal population centers.

Foreign Travel: The law does not permit those under age 18 to travel abroad without a guardian's permission. Married women under 18 may not travel abroad without permission from their husbands, but married women over 18 may do so.

The government did not permit young men eligible for the draft, who had not completed their military service, to leave the country without special authorization, although the government granted such authorization to students and persons with special family circumstances. The Ministry of Interior affirmed that in 2014 the government ended its requirement for background checks on passport applicants.

Protection of Refugees

The government provided protection to an estimated 90,000 to 165,000 Sahrawi refugees who departed Western Sahara after Morocco took control of the territory in the 1970s. UNHCR, the World Food Program (WFP), the Algerian Red Crescent, the Sahrawi Red Crescent, and other organizations also assisted Sahrawi refugees. Neither the government nor the refugee leadership allowed UNHCR to conduct registration or complete a census of the Sahrawi refugees. In the absence of formal registration, UNHCR and the WFP based humanitarian assistance on a planning figure of 90,000 refugees with an additional 35,000 supplementary food rations.

Access to Asylum: While the law provides generally for asylum or refugee status, the government has not established a formal system through which refugees can request asylum. There were no reports that the government granted refugee status and asylum to new refugee applicants during the year. According to UNHCR, the government did not accept UNHCR-determined refugee status for individuals. UNHCR offices in Algiers reported an estimated 200 to 300 asylum requests per month, mostly from Syrian, Palestinian, and sub-Saharan African individuals coming from Mali, Guinea, Central African Republic, Cote d'Ivoire, and the Democratic Republic of the Congo (DRC). Those determined by UNHCR to have valid refugee claims were primarily from the DRC, Cote d'Ivoire, Iraq, and the Central African Republic. There was no evidence of any pattern of discrimination toward asylum applicants, but the lack of a formal asylum system made this difficult to assess.

As of September 2015 the Ministry of National Solidarity, Family, and the Status of Women reported that since the start of the conflict in Syria, it accepted more than 24,000 Syrian refugees. Other organizations estimated the number to be closer to 43,000 Syrians. Starting in January 2015 the government instituted visa requirements for Syrians entering the country. Since 2012 UNHCR registered more than 6,000 Syrians, but only approximately 5,000 remained registered with UNHCR as of September. The Algerian Red Crescent, which is subordinate to the Ministry of Solidarity, maintained "welcome facilities" that provided food and shelter for those Syrians without means to support themselves. The facilities were located at a summer camp in the seaside area of Algiers known as Sidi Fredj. The government did not grant UNHCR access to these reception centers but reported that by 2016 most Syrians no longer used the centers.

Since the outbreak of violence in northern Mali in 2012, international observers reported an influx of individuals into Algeria across the Malian border inconsistent with traditional migratory movements.

The Ministry of Interior estimated in August that there were 21,073 illegal migrants residing in the country, while other sources assessed there were 30,000 in Tamanrasset alone and as many as 100,000 in the country. As of July the Algerian Red Crescent had closed all four of the refugee camps it had been managing, including its camp housing 600 migrants, mostly from Mali, near the southern city of Bordj Badj Mokhtar.

Refoulement: The government provided some protection against the expulsion or return of refugees to countries where their lives or freedom would be threatened because of their race, religion, nationality, membership in a particular social group, or political opinion. In early December, however, the government gathered an estimated 1,400 sub-Saharan migrants in communities outside of Algiers and removed nearly 1,000 of them to Niger. The president of the Algerian Red Crescent said all returns were voluntary, adding that some migrants were permitted to remain in Tamanrasset. The removals followed a period of several years in which the government had largely refrained from deporting sub-Saharan migrants due to security concerns and the instability in northern Mali.

The government, led by the Algerian Red Crescent, repatriated a total of more than 17,000 Nigerien migrants to their country at the request of the government of Niger since 2014, in several repatriation operations. Various international humanitarian organizations and observers criticized the operations, citing unacceptable conditions of transport, primarily on the Niger side of the border, and what they described as a lack of coordination between the Algerian Red Crescent and the government and Red Cross of Niger. Observers also questioned whether all of the migrants were voluntarily repatriated. In August the government arranged the repatriation of approximately 500 Malians per a request from the Malian consulate in Tamanrasset.

Employment: UNHCR provided registered refugees with modest food assistance and lodging support. Because the government does not formally allow refugee employment, many worked in the informal market and were at risk of labor exploitation due to their lack of legal status in the country. Other migrants, asylum seekers, and Malians and Syrians who had a "special status" with the government, relied largely on remittances from family, the support of local family and acquaintances, and assistance from the Algerian Red Crescent and international aid organizations.

Access to Basic Services: Sahrawi refugees lived predominantly in five camps near the city of Tindouf, administered by the Popular Front for the Liberation of the Saguia el Harma and Rio de Oro (Polisario). The Polisario (through the Sahrawi Red Crescent Society), UNHCR, WFP, the UN Children's Fund (UNICEF), and partner NGOs largely provided basic services including food aid, primary health care, and primary and secondary education, while the government invested heavily in developing the camps' infrastructure and also provided free secondary and university educations, as well as advanced hospital care, to Sahrawi refugees. The remote location of the camps and lack of government presence resulted in a lack of access by police and courts. Other refugees, asylum seekers, and migrants had access to free public hospitals, but independent NGOs reported instances of migrants turned away.

In August 2015 the Ministry of Education instructed all school administrators to allow migrant and refugee children to enroll in primary school through high school and require only that they present their passport and documentation showing their level of schooling from their home country. International organizations reported the children had trouble in their attempts to integrate into the educational system but that migrants' access to education was improving, particularly in the north of the country. These organizations reported that migrant parents were often reluctant to enroll their children in Algerian schools.

Durable Solutions: The government did not accept refugees from foreign countries for resettlement. The Sahrawi refugees had not sought local integration or naturalization during their 40-year stay in the refugee camps near Tindouf, and their ruling party, the Polisario, continued to call for a referendum on independence in Western Sahara.

Temporary Protection: The law does not address formal temporary protection, but authorities provided informal, temporary protection to groups such as Syrians and Malians.

Section 3. Freedom to Participate in the Political Process

The constitution provides citizens the ability to choose their government in free and fair periodic elections held by secret ballot and based on universal and equal suffrage. Restrictions on freedom of assembly and association as well as restrictions on political party activities greatly inhibited the activity of opposition groups.

Elections and Political Participation

The law states that members of local, provincial, and national assemblies are elected for five-year mandates and that presidential elections occur within 30 days prior to the expiration of the presidential mandate. Presidential term limits, which were eliminated in 2008, were reintroduced in a 2016 revision of the constitution and limit the president to two terms. The Ministry of Interior maintains oversight of the election and voting processes. Legislation passed by parliament in July established an independent electoral monitoring body. The president appointed the head of the monitoring body on November 6, but as of November the other members had not been appointed.

Recent Elections: Presidential elections took place in April 2014, and voters re-elected President Bouteflika for a fourth term. Although he did not personally campaign, Bouteflika won approximately 81 percent of the votes, while his main rival and former prime minister, Ali Benflis, placed second with slightly more than 12 percent.

Several hundred international election observers from the United Nations, Arab League, African Union, and Organization of Islamic Cooperation monitored voting. Foreign observers characterized the elections as largely peaceful but pointed to low voter turnout and a high rate of ballot invalidity. *El Watan*, an opposition-leaning daily newspaper, reported that almost 10 percent of ballots cast were invalid. The Ministry of Interior did not provide domestic or foreign observers with voter registration lists. The president of the Constitutional Council, Mourad Medelci, announced voter participation in the elections was just under 51 percent, a sharp drop from the slightly more than 74 percent turnout during the previous presidential election in 2009.

Ali Benflis rejected the results and claimed that fraud marred the elections. He appealed to the Constitutional Council without result. A coalition of Islamic and secular opposition parties boycotted the election, describing it as a masquerade and asserting that President Bouteflika was unfit to run due to his health. Several candidates withdrew from the race, claiming that the outcome was a foregone conclusion.

Elections for the lower chamber of parliament were held in 2012 and did not result in significant changes in the composition of the government. The government allowed international observation of the elections but did not permit local civil society organizations to do the same. Several opposition parties subsequently boycotted the opening session of parliament, alleging fraud during the elections.

Political Parties and Political Participation: The Ministry of Interior must approve political parties before they may operate legally.

The government maintained undue media influence and opposition political parties claimed they did not have access to public television and radio. Security forces dispersed political opposition rallies and interfered with the right to organize.

Pursuant to the constitution, all parties must have a "national base." Under the previous electoral law, a party must have received 4 percent of the vote or at least 2,000 votes in 25 provinces in one of the last three legislative elections to participate in national elections, making it very difficult to create new political parties. The new electoral law adopted by parliament in July requires parties to have received 4 percent of the vote in the preceding election or to collect 250 signatures in the electoral district in order to appear on the ballot. Opposition parties from across the political spectrum criticized the new law for creating a more stringent qualification threshold for parties, as well as for establishing an electoral monitoring body whose members would be appointed by the president and parliament, which is controlled by a coalition headed by the president's party.

The law prohibits parties based on religion, ethnicity, gender, language, or region, but there were various political parties commonly known to be Islamist, notably members of the Green Alliance. According to the Ministry of Interior, in August there were 71 registered political parties.

The law does not place significant restrictions on voter registration, but implementation of voter registration and identification laws proved inconsistent and confusing during past elections.

Membership in the Islamic Salvation Front, a political party banned since 1992, remained illegal. The law also bans political party ties to nonpolitical associations and regulates party financing and reporting requirements. According to the law, political parties may not receive direct or indirect financial or material support from any foreign parties. The law also stipulates the collection of resources from contributions by the party's members, donations, and revenue from its activities, in addition to possible state funding.

As of September parliamentarian and founder of the Democratic and Social Union (UDS) party, Karim Tabbou, awaited authorization from the Ministry of Interior to hold his party's congress. Originally scheduled in 2014, the UDS could not hold its congress because the party had not received the authorization for its required regional congresses.

In August a local government official in Tamanrasset sent the Rally for Culture and Democracy (RCD) political party a letter stating it may decline to authorize future RCD meetings after a gathering of RCD youth members turned disorderly. The party denied the allegation of disorderliness, asserting instead that security personnel were displeased because of the presence of an Amazigh flag beside the Algerian national flag and because organizers removed a portrait of President Bouteflika from the meeting hall.

On July 16 and September 17, the media reported that police prevented members of the ruling National Liberation Front (FLN) party, including members of parliament, from gathering. On both occasions party members who opposed the party's secretary general planned to meet at the home of Senator Boualam Djaafar. The online news site *Tout sur L'Algerie* reported that Abderrahmane Belayat, a former minister and FLN secretary general who was a member of the group, said the intelligence services regularly monitored the group's meetings.

<u>Participation of Women and Minorities</u>: No laws limit the participation of women and members of minorities in the political process, and women and minorities did participate.

Section 4. Corruption and Lack of Transparency in Government

The law provides for criminal penalties of two to 10 years in prison for official corruption, but the government generally did not implement the law effectively. Corruption remained a problem as reflected in the Transparency International corruption index.

<u>Corruption</u>: The criminal code stipulates that charges related to theft, embezzlement, or loss of public and private funds may be initiated against senior,

public sector "economic managers" only by the board of directors of the institution. Critics of the law asserted that by permitting only senior officials of state businesses to initiate investigations, the law protects high-level government corruption and promotes impunity.

The Ministry of Justice declared that as of October, 987 government employees or employees of state-run businesses had been charged with corruption-related offenses. The government brought several major corruption cases to trial, resulting in dozens of convictions. Media reporting and public opinion viewed the absence of charges against the most senior of government officials as an indication of impunity for government officials.

In July the International Consortium of Investigative Journalists (ICIJ) published an article based on the "Panama Papers," leaked documents from Panama-based law firm Mossack Fonseca, related to allegations of bribery in connection with contracts awarded by Sonatrach, the national oil company. The ICIJ said the documents demonstrated that Mossack Fonseca created 12 of the 17 shell companies established by businessman Farid Bedjaoui for the alleged purpose of funneling bribes to government officials. Former energy minister Chekib Khelil, who had previously been under a 2013 international arrest warrant to face charges in Algeria in connection with the case, returned to Algeria in March after charges were dropped. Former minister of justice Mohamed Charfi claimed he was pressured by FLN secretary general Amar Saadani in 2013 to drop charges against Khelil shortly before he was removed from his post.

On February 2, a court sentenced 12 persons to sentences ranging from 18-month suspended jail terms to six years in prison in a corruption case involving Sonatrach contracting practices. Former Sonatrach CEO Mohamed Meziane received a suspended six-year sentence, and two of his sons were sentenced to five and six years' imprisonment.

Corruption throughout the government stemmed largely from the bloated nature of the bureaucracy and a lack of transparent oversight. The CNCPPDH stated in its 2014 annual report that public corruption remained a problem and hindered development. The National Association for the Fight Against Corruption noted the existence of an effective anticorruption law but stated that the government lacked the "political will" to apply the law.

Financial Disclosure: The law stipulates that all elected government officials and those appointed by presidential decree must declare their assets the month they commence their jobs, if there is substantial change in their wealth while they are in office, and at the end of their term. Few government officials made their personal wealth public, and there was no enforcement of the law.

Public Access to Information: Lack of government transparency remained a serious problem. Most ministries had websites, but not all ministries regularly maintained them with updated information. Analysts, academics, and other interested parties often had difficulty obtaining even routine and nominally public economic data from government ministries.

Section 5. Governmental Attitude Regarding International and Nongovernmental Investigation of Alleged Violations of Human Rights

A variety of domestic human rights groups operated with varying degrees of government restriction and cooperation. The law requires all civil associations to apply for operating permission, and at year's end several major civil associations remained unrecognized but tolerated.

AI maintained an office and actively reported on human rights issues, but it did not receive official authorization to operate from the Ministry of Interior.

Although the government did not renew the accreditation of LADDH, the organization had members countrywide, received independent funding, and was the most active independent human rights group. The smaller Algerian League for Human Rights, a separate but licensed organization based in Constantine, had members throughout the country monitoring individual cases.

The United Nations or Other International Bodies: The government extended an invitation to the UN Working Group on Enforced or Involuntary Disappearances in 2014 and again in September 2015, but as of September no visit occurred. The country joined the UN Human Rights Council in 2014 but continued to deny requests for visits from the UN special rapporteurs on extrajudicial executions (pending since 1998) and on human rights and counterterrorism (pending since 2006) and the UN Working Group on arbitrary detention (pending since 2009).

Government Human Rights Bodies: The CNCPPDH plays a consultative and advisory role to the government. It issues an annual report on the status of human rights in the country. Published in July, the 2015 report highlighted government advances in social and legal rights with increased protections for women and children, the introduction of mediation in nonfelony criminal cases, and limits on the use of pretrial detention. The commission identified its principal concerns as public corruption, shortfalls in the recent law on violence against women, heavy bureaucracy, and impediments limiting citizens' access to justice.

Section 6. Discrimination, Societal Abuses, and Trafficking in Persons

Women

Rape and Domestic Violence: Rape, both spousal and nonspousal, occurred. The law criminalizes nonspousal rape but does not address spousal rape. Prison sentences for nonspousal rape range from five to 10 years, and authorities generally enforced the law. Many women did not report incidents of rape because of societal and family pressures. The CNCPPDH's 2015 report called on the government to repeal the provision of the penal code that allows someone accused of raping a minor to avoid prosecution if he subsequently marries his victim.

Domestic violence was widespread. The law states that a person claiming domestic abuse must visit a "forensic physician" for an examination to document injuries and that the physician must determine that the victim suffered from injuries that "incapacitated" the person for 15 days. The law also requires that the physician provide the victim with a "certificate of incapacity" attesting to the injuries, which the victim presents to authorities as the basis of the criminal complaint. The government, working with the UN Population Fund, undertook a public awareness campaign to inform women of their rights under the law, encourage reporting of domestic violence, and engage men in conversations on violence against women.

According to statistics released by the Ministry of Justice, between the beginning of 2015 and June 2016, there were 14,366 cases of domestic abuse, of which 12,804 involved male perpetrators. As of October, 10,536 of the cases had resulted in convictions. The government said that most of those convicted received prison time as well as a fine. According to statistics from women's advocacy groups published in the local press, between 100 and 200 women died each year from domestic violence.

The Information and Documentation Center on the Rights of Children and Women (CIDDEF), a network of local organizations that promoted the rights of women, managed call centers in 15 provinces and reported that each center received 300-400 calls during the year from female victims of violence seeking assistance.

The law provides for sentences of one to 20 years' imprisonment for domestic violence and six months' to two years' incarceration for men who withhold property or financial resources from their spouses. While supporting the law when it was drafted, AI and domestic women's rights groups criticized its "forgiveness" clause that permits the annulment of charges if the abused spouse pardons her husband.

Sexual Harassment: The punishment for sexual harassment is one to two years' imprisonment and a fine of DZD 50,000 to DZD 100,000 ($458 to $916); the punishment doubles for a second offense. Women's groups reported that official statistics on harassment were not available but that the majority of reported cases of harassment occurred in the workplace. Women also reported harassment by men when walking in public. The government acknowledged that street harassment continued to be a problem despite advances in the law.

Reproductive Rights: Couples and individuals have the right to decide the number, timing, and spacing of their children; manage their reproductive health; and have access to the information and means to do so, with limited societal discrimination and coercion. Conservative elements of society challenged the government's family planning program, including the provision of free contraception. Married and unmarried women had access to contraceptives, although there were reports of pharmacists who refused to sell contraception to unmarried women. A study by a prominent women's group in 2015 found that approximately 68 to 70 percent of women used contraception, the majority of whom took birth control pills. Women did not need permission to obtain birth control pills, but doctors required permission of the partner for women who sought tubal ligation.

Societal and family pressure restricted women from making independent decisions about their health and reproductive rights.

Discrimination: Although the constitution provides for gender equality, many aspects of the law and traditional social practices discriminated against women. In addition, religious extremists advocated practices that led to restrictions on women's behavior, including freedom of movement. In some rural regions, women faced extreme social pressure to veil as a precondition for freedom of movement and employment. In September a security guard at a high school in Algiers reportedly prevented unveiled students from entering the school on the first day of classes. The law contains traditional elements of Islamic law. It prohibits Muslim women from marrying non-Muslims, although authorities did not always enforce this provision. Muslim men may marry non-Muslim women. A woman may marry a foreigner and transmit citizenship and nationality to both her children and spouse.

Women may seek divorce for irreconcilable differences and violation of a prenuptial agreement. In a divorce the law provides for the wife to retain the family's home until children reach age 18. Authorities normally awarded custody of children to the mother, but she may not make decisions about education or take the children out of the country without the father's authorization. Women were more likely to retain the family's home if they had custody of the children. In January 2015 the government created a subsidy for divorced women whose ex-husbands failed to make child support payments.

The law affirms the religiously based practice of allowing a man to marry as many as four wives. The law permits polygamy only upon the agreement of the first wife and the determination of a judge as to the husband's financial ability to support an additional wife. A joint Ministry of Health and UN study from 2013 estimated that 3 percent of marriages were polygamous. It was unclear whether authorities followed the law in all cases.

Amendments to the law supersede the religiously based requirement that a male sponsor consent to the marriage of a woman. The sponsor represents the woman during the religious or civil ceremony. Although the law formally retains the requirement of a sponsor to contract the marriage, the woman may choose any man that she wishes to be her sponsor. Some families subjected women to virginity tests before marriage.

Women suffered from discrimination in inheritance claims and were entitled to a smaller portion of an estate than male children or a deceased husband's brothers. Women did not often have exclusive control over assets that they brought to a marriage or that they earned. Women may take out business loans and use their own financial resources. Women enjoyed rights equal to those of men concerning property ownership, and property titles listed female landowners' names.

Women faced discrimination in employment. Leaders of women's organizations reported that discrimination was common and women were less likely to receive equal pay for equal work or promotions. In urban areas there was social encouragement for women to pursue higher education or a career. Girls graduated from high school and attended university more frequently than boys.

According to a study released by CIDDEF, women represented 19.5 percent of the active workforce, with 61 percent of these women working in the public sector. As of September 2015, female unemployment was higher than that of men, with 16.6 percent of women unemployed compared to 9.9 percent of men, according to a National Office of Statistics report. While the presence of women in the workforce grew, access to management positions remained limited. Women served at all levels in the judicial system. The government employed an increasing number of female police, including approximately 6 percent of DGSN police officers. Women may own businesses, enter into contracts, and pursue careers similar to those of men.

Children

Birth registration: The mother or father may transmit citizenship and nationality. By law children born to a Muslim father are Muslim, regardless of the mother's religion. The law did not differentiate between girls and boys in registration of birth.

Education: Education was free, compulsory, and universal through the secondary level to age 16. UNICEF reported that the attendance of girls was higher in secondary school due to instances of boys leaving school after the primary level. The United Nations estimated primary school enrollment at more than 97 percent. The government estimated that during the 2014-15 school year, children under the age of six were enrolled in school at a rate of 98.49 percent, with those between the ages of six and 16 enrolled at a rate of 95 percent.

Child Abuse: Child abuse is illegal but was a serious problem to which the government devoted increasing resources and attention. In June the government appointed a national ombudsperson responsible for monitoring and publishing an annual report on the rights of children. The government supported the country's Network for the Defense of Children's Rights (NADA). Experts assumed that many cases went unreported because of family reticence. The head of NADA reported that the NGO's free helpline received more than 23,000 calls requesting assistance as of August. The DGSN reported 1,663 cases of child sexual abuse in 2014, and the National Gendarmerie reported 380 cases.

Kidnapping for any reason is a crime. Laws prohibiting parental abduction do not penalize mothers and fathers differently. In 2014 legislation increased the punishment for convicted kidnappers to include the death penalty. The DGSN commissioner for the National Office of Child Protection reported the kidnapping of 28 children for the period of January through August, compared with 84 in 2015.

<u>Early and Forced Marriage</u>: The legal minimum age of marriage is 19 for both men and women, but minors may marry with parental consent, regardless of gender. The law forbids legal guardians from forcing minors under their care to marry against the minor's will. The Ministry of Religious Affairs required that couples present a government-issued marriage certificate before permitting imams to conduct religious marriage ceremonies.

<u>Sexual Exploitation of Children</u>: The law prohibits solicitation for prostitution and stipulates prison sentences of between 10 and 20 years when the offense is committed against a minor under age 18. By law the age for consensual sex is 16. The law stipulates a prison sentence of between 10 and 20 years for rape when the victim is a minor. The law does not call for prosecuting a man accused of raping a female minor if he legally marries the victim, and there were no available reports of this practice during the year. The law prohibits pornography and establishes prison sentences from two months to two years as well as fines up to DZD 2,000 ($18).

A 2015 law created a national council to address children's issues, improved social services and protection for children, gave judges authority to remove children from an abusive home, and allowed sexually abused children to provide testimony on video rather than in court.

<u>International Child Abductions</u>: The country is not a party to the 1980 Hague Convention on the Civil Aspects of International Child Abduction. See the Department of State's *Annual Report on International Parental Child Abduction* at travel.state.gov/content/childabduction/en/legal/compliance.html.

Anti-Semitism

Some religious leaders estimated that the country's Jewish population numbered fewer than 200 persons. Local Jewish community leaders estimated the number to be in the low hundreds. The media did not publish any known derogatory political cartoons or articles directed at the Jewish community, but observers found anti-Semitic postings on social media sites.

Jewish leaders reported that the Jewish community faced unofficial, religion-based obstacles to government employment and administrative difficulties when working with government bureaucracy.

In May a member of parliament affiliated with the Islamist Green Alliance criticized the government for granting a visa to an Israeli journalist accompanying the French prime minister on an April visit to Algeria. An Arabic-language newspaper wrote that the journalist had a "strong Jewish-sounding name" and stated that, in the member of parliament's view, the government was normalizing relations with "Zionists who make France a door to infiltrate" Algeria. An online news outlet referred to the journalist as an "Israeli Jew" and stated that the visa allowed him to "strut in the streets of Algiers to meet whoever he wants."

Trafficking in Persons

See the Department of State's *Trafficking in Persons Report* at www.state.gov/j/tip/rls/tiprpt/.

Persons with Disabilities

The law prohibits discrimination against persons with disabilities in employment, education, access to health care, or the provision of other state services, although the government did not effectively enforce these provisions. Persons with disabilities faced widespread social discrimination. Few government buildings were accessible to persons with disabilities. Few businesses abided by the law that they reserve 1 percent of jobs for persons with disabilities. Business that did not meet the 1 percent quota received a DZD 140,000 ($1,282) fine. NGOs reported that the government did not enforce payment of fines. The Ministry of National Solidarity, Family, and the Status of Women provided some financial support to health-care-oriented NGOs, but for many NGOs, such financial support represented a small fraction of their budgets. The ministry also provided disability benefits to persons with disabilities who registered with the government. Social security provided payments for orthopedic equipment.

The Ministry of Solidarity reported that it ran 222 centers throughout the country that provided support for persons with intellectual, auditory, vision, and physical disabilities. The ministry stated that it worked in concert with the Ministry of Education to integrate children with disabilities into public schools to promote inclusion. The majority of the ministry's programs for children with disabilities remained in social centers for children with disabilities rather than in formal educational institutions. Advocacy groups reported that children with disabilities rarely attended school past the secondary level. Many schools lacked teachers trained to work with children with disabilities, threatening the viability of efforts to mainstream children with disabilities into public schools. Numerous private schools existed but, according to advocacy organizations, staff often acted more as caretakers than teachers due to a lack of training.

Many persons with disabilities faced challenges in voting due to voting centers that lacked accessible features.

Acts of Violence, Discrimination, and Other Abuses Based on Sexual Orientation and Gender Identity

The law criminalizes public and consensual same-sex sexual relations by men or women with penalties that include imprisonment of six months to three years and a fine of DZD 1,000 to DZD 10,000 ($9 to $92). The law also stipulates penalties that include imprisonment of two months to two years and fines of DZD 500 to DZD 2,000 ($5 to $18) for anyone convicted of having committed a "homosexual act." If a minor is involved, the adult may face up to three years' imprisonment and a fine of DZD 10,000 ($92).

LGBTI activists reported that the vague wording of laws identifying "homosexual acts" and "acts against nature" permitted sweeping accusations that resulted during the year in multiple arrests for same-sex sexual relations but no known prosecutions.

LGBTI persons faced strong societal and religious discrimination. While some lived openly, the vast majority did not, and most feared reprisal from their families or harassment from authorities. One activist reported that of the 100 LGBTI persons he knew, only three had "come out." During a May 2015 radio interview, Minister of Religious Affairs Mohamed Aissa said that combatting individuals who promote the deviation of morality and the dismantling of the family (a reference to the behavior of LGBTI individuals) was more important than the fight against Da'esh.

Activists said that the government did not actively punish LGBTI behavior, but it was complicit in the hate speech propagated by conservative, cultural, and religion-based organizations, some of which associated LGBTI individuals with pedophiles and encouraged excluding them from family and society. Trans Homos DZ, a local organization that advocated for the rights of LGBTI persons, published a report on anti-LGBTI hate speech in the media, detailing several incidents from recent years including programs broadcast by Arabic-language media outlets, such as Ennahar TV and Echourouk TV, that demonized LGBTI persons. The report also detailed social media and other online hate speech directed at the LGBTI community between 2013 and 2015. The organization reported in April that two men who used homophobic slurs physically attacked an activist who supported LGBTI rights in Algiers. In another incident a video posted on YouTube in November 2015 showed what appeared to be a group of men surrounding a transgender woman on the street. Several of the men were shown kicking and punching her while others looked on without intervening. The government did not announce investigations into the perpetrators of either alleged attack.

Another report released by Trans Homos DZ in November included allegations by an anonymous former prisoner alleging that prisoners at El Harrach Prison suffered physical and sexual abuse based on their sexual orientation. The former prisoner's report said prisoners who were perceived as gay or transgender were placed in a specific cellblock near other prisoners who had committed serious crimes. The report said gay and transgender prisoners were frequently victims of sexual assaults, including one incident in which prison guards mocked and initially refused medical treatment to a prisoner who was the victim of a gang rape.

Due to the hacking of one LGBTI organization's website in 2015 and increased offensive and derogatory media coverage specifically denouncing LGBTI practices, activists reported the need to focus their advocacy on personal safety and minimized their activities during the year. Activists reported that members of the LGBTI community declined to report abuse and thus lessened their capacity to report cases of homophobic abuse and rape due to fear of reprisal by authorities. Reporting that access to health services could be difficult because medical personnel often treated LGBTI patients unprofessionally, activists noted that some organizations maintained a list of "LGBTI-friendly" hospitals, and several NGOs operated mobile clinics specifically for vulnerable communities.

Employers refused jobs to LGBTI persons, particularly men perceived as effeminate. Activists also reported cases of individuals denied drivers licenses due to their perceived sexual orientation. Community members said that obtaining legal assistance was also a challenge due to similar discrimination. Members of the LGBTI community reported that forced marriage was a problem, particularly for lesbians.

Alouen, an Oran-based LGBTI advocacy group, continued cyberactivism on behalf of the LGBTI community.

HIV and AIDS Social Stigma

HIV/AIDS was widely considered a shameful disease. There were more reported cases in men than women, with the exception of women between ages 15 and 24. The government continued to offer free antiretroviral treatment to all persons, including migrants. Authorities virtually eliminated new HIV infections among children. The Joint UN Program on HIV/AIDS (UNAIDS) reported the existence of more than 2,000 centers offering free testing and counseling services, 1,500 of which the government managed. Strong social stigma towards the vulnerable groups in which HIV/AIDS was most concentrated--commercial sex workers, men who have sexual relations with men, and drug users--deterred testing of these groups. A 2014 study found a 5 percent prevalence rate of HIV/AIDS among commercial sex workers in Oran, the country's second largest city. Another NGO reported the prevalence rate of the same community at nearly 10 percent.

A Ministry of Health report found that there were 740 new cases of HIV/AIDS in 2015, contributing to an official estimate of 9,843 persons with HIV/AIDS. The government provided treatment to 7,915 individuals in 2015. UNAIDS estimated that 8,800 persons had HIV/AIDS in 2015, 300 of whom were under age 15.

Led by the Ministry of Health, the government established the National AIDS Committee, which met twice during the first eight months of the year. The committee brought together various government and civil society actors to discuss implementation of the national strategy to combat HIV/AIDS.

The Green Tea Association, an NGO working in the field of HIV/AIDS treatment, continued to operate an information and orientation center in Tamanrasset, a province known for its large and diverse population of migrants.

Other Societal Violence or Discrimination

Clashes between Algerian citizens and sub-Saharan migrants in March injured dozens of persons in Ouargla and Bechar and prompted the government to relocate more than 1,000 migrants to other locations in the country (see section 2). In Ouargla press reported that Algerians attacked Malian and Nigerien migrants on March 2 after learning that a sub-Saharan migrant had broken into a house and fatally stabbed an Algerian man. On March 25, dozens of reportedly masked men in Bechar threw stones and other objects at migrants in response to allegations that a migrant was involved in an attempted rape of a child.

Section 7. Worker Rights

a. Freedom of Association and the Right to Collective Bargaining

The constitution provides workers with the right to join and form unions of their choice provided they are citizens. The country has ratified the International Labor Organization's (ILO) conventions on freedom of association and collective bargaining but failed to enact legislation needed to implement these conventions fully.

The law requires that workers obtain government approval to form a union, and the Ministry of Labor must approve or disapprove a union application within 30 days. To found a union, an applicant must be Algerian by birth or have held Algerian nationality for 10 years. The law also provides for the creation of independent unions, although the union's membership must account for at least 20 percent of an enterprise's workforce. Unions have the right to form and join federations or confederations, and the government recognized four confederations. Unions may recruit members at the workplace. The law prohibits discrimination by employers against union members and organizers and provides mechanisms for resolving trade union complaints of antiunion practices by employers.

The law permits unions to affiliate with international labor bodies and develop relations with foreign labor groups. For example, the General Union of Algerian Workers (UGTA), which represented a majority of public-sector workers, is an affiliate of the International Trade Union Confederation. Nevertheless, the law prohibits unions from associating with political parties and receiving funds from foreign sources. The courts are empowered to dissolve unions that engage in illegal activities. The government may invalidate a union's legal status if authorities perceive its objectives to be contrary to the established institutional system, public order, good morals, law, or regulations in force.

The law provides for collective bargaining by all unions, and the government permitted the exercise of this right for authorized unions. Nevertheless, the UGTA remained the only union authorized to negotiate collective bargaining agreements.

The law provides for the right to strike, and workers exercised this right, subject to conditions. Striking requires a secret ballot of the whole workforce. The decision to strike must be approved by majority vote of workers at a general meeting. The government may restrict strikes on a number of grounds, including economic crisis, obstruction of public services, or the possibility of subversive actions. Furthermore, all public demonstrations, including protests and strikes, must receive prior government authorization. By law workers may strike only after 14 days of mandatory conciliation or mediation. The government occasionally offered to mediate disputes. The law states that decisions reached in mediation are binding on both parties. If mediation does not lead to an agreement, workers may strike legally after they vote by secret ballot to do so. The law requires that a minimum level of essential public services must be maintained during public-sector service strikes, and the government has broad legal authority to requisition public employees. The list of essential services included services such as banking, radio, and television. Penalties for unlawful work stoppages range from eight days to two months' imprisonment.

The government affirmed there were 101 registered trade unions and employer's organizations. No new trade unions were registered between January and August. Many trade unions remained unrecognized by the government; they identified delayed processing and administrative hurdles imposed by the government as the primary obstacles to establishing legal status. In June the ILO Committee of Experts on the Application of Conventions and Recommendations stated that the lengthy registration process seriously impedes the establishment of new unions.

Attempts by new unions to form federations or confederations suffered similar challenges. Representatives of the National Autonomous Union for Public Administration Personnel (SNAPAP) stated that the union continued to function without official status.

Formed in 2013 but not recognized by the government, the General Autonomous Confederation of Workers in Algeria (CGATA) included public and economic sector unions and committees. In March 2015 the Ministry of Labor refused to register CGATA as a national confederation, thus preventing it from establishing an independent multisector confederation that would include private sector employees. CGATA membership included workers from unions representing government administrators, diplomatic personnel, state electricity and gas employees, university professors, public transport and postal workers, and lawyers. The confederation also included migrants working in the country.

SNAPAP and other independent unions faced government interference throughout the year, including official obstruction of general assembly meetings and police harassment during sit-in protests. Furthermore, unions in multi-national companies, specifically in oil and gas production, were virtually nonexistent due to antiunion practices, threats, and harassment by employers.

In April police stopped hundreds of protesting teachers in Boudouaou, preventing them from completing a union-organized march into Algiers. Authorities reportedly jammed mobile networks in the area and blocked deliveries of food and drink to the protest site. Teachers' union members said police grabbed and shoved protesters during an attempt to break up the protest.

On February 6, police surrounded a trade union office in Bab Ezzouar, where a meeting was planned to discuss the 2016 finance law. Press reported that police arrested six activists and union members, including Salah Debouz, for assembling without a permit.

The Committee of Experts at the International Labor Conference in June requested that the government reinstate employees that the committee determined were fired based on antiunion discrimination and act expeditiously to process pending trade union registration applications.

Antiunion intimidation was commonplace, and there were several strikes launched in reaction to the government's refusal to extend official recognition to fledgling new unions and its practice of engaging only with the UGTA. In March the ILO Committee on Freedom of Association urged the government to reinstate two Autonomous National Union of Postal Workers officials, in compliance with a court order. The committee concluded that the governmental postal system improperly dismissed the two officials in 2014 in connection with statements they made to the media and with one official's role in organizing a work stoppage.

b. Prohibition of Forced or Compulsory Labor

The law prohibits all forms of human trafficking. There were reports from NGOs that such practices occurred. Forced labor conditions existed for migrant workers, and the law did not fully protect them. For example, female migrants were subjected to debt bondage as they worked to repay smuggling debts through domestic servitude, forced begging, and forced prostitution. Prescribed penalties under this statute range from three to 20 years' imprisonment, which are sufficiently stringent and commensurate with those prescribed for other serious crimes, such as rape. Construction workers and domestic workers were reportedly vulnerable. The government made limited efforts to prosecute traffickers and protect victims but created an interministerial committee to coordinate antitrafficking efforts and adopted a national antitrafficking action plan.

Also see the Department of State's *Trafficking in Persons Report* at www.state.gov/j/tip/rls/tiprpt/.

c. Prohibition of Child Labor and Minimum Age for Employment

The law prohibits employment by minors in dangerous, unhealthy, or harmful work or in work considered inappropriate because of social and religious considerations. The minimum legal age for employment is 16, but younger children may work as apprentices with permission from their parents or legal guardian. The law prohibits workers under age 19 from working at night.

Although specific data was unavailable, children reportedly worked mostly in the informal sales market, often in family businesses. There were isolated reports that children were subjected to commercial sexual exploitation (see section 6, Children). According to UNICEF, 5 percent of children ages five to 14 were economically active.

The Ministry of Labor is responsible for enforcing child labor laws and refers violators to the Ministry of Justice for prosecution. There is no single office charged with this task, but all labor inspectors are responsible for enforcing laws regarding child labor. The Ministry of Labor conducted inspections and in some cases investigated companies suspected of hiring underage workers. The ministry's Labor Inspector Service conducted an investigation into child labor in 2015 of 15,093 businesses from the trade, agriculture, construction, and services industries. It reported the discovery of 97 minors, of whom 47 were under the age of 16. The law for the protection of the child, adopted in 2015, criminalizes anyone who economically exploits a child with a penalty of one to three years' imprisonment and a fine of DZD 50,000 to DZD 100,000 ($476 to $952); the punishment is doubled if the offender is a family member or guardian of the child. These penalties are neither sufficiently stringent nor commensurate with those prescribed for other serious crimes, such as rape. Monitoring and enforcement practices for child labor were inconsistent and hampered by an insufficient number of inspectors.

The Ministry of Solidarity leads a national committee composed of 12 ministries and NGOs that meets yearly to discuss child labor issues. The committee was empowered to propose measures and laws to address child labor as well as conduct awareness campaigns.

d. Discrimination with Respect to Employment and Occupation

The law prohibits discrimination with respect to employment, salary, and work environment based on age, gender, social and marital status, family links, political conviction, disability, national origin and affiliation with a union. The law does not prohibit discrimination with respect to employment based on sexual orientation, HIV-positive status, or religion. The government did not adequately enforce the law, since discrimination reportedly existed, specifically against migrant workers in the informal economy who lacked a legal means to address unfair working conditions.

Women occupied few decision-making positions. Many unescorted or migrant female youth were exploited as domestic workers and were known to be loaned out to families for extended periods to work in homes and/or exploited as prostitutes (see section 6).

e. Acceptable Conditions of Work

A tripartite social pact among business, government, and the official union established the national minimum wage of DZD 18,000 ($165) per month in 2012. The World Bank estimated in 2011 that the poverty rate was 5.5 percent, a level that some observers considered too low.

The standard workweek was 40 hours, including one hour for lunch per day. Half of the lunch hour is considered compensated working time. Employees who worked longer than the standard workweek received premium pay on a sliding scale from time-and-a-half to double time, depending on whether the overtime occurred on a normal workday, a weekend, or a holiday.

The law contains occupational health and safety standards that were not fully enforced. There were no known reports of workers dismissed for removing themselves from hazardous working conditions. If workers face such conditions, they may reserve the right to renegotiate their contract or, failing that, resort to the courts. While this legal mechanism exists, the high demand for employment in the country gave an advantage to employers seeking to exploit employees. Labor standards do not protect economic migrants from sub-Saharan Africa and elsewhere working in the country without legal immigration status, which made them vulnerable to exploitation. The law does not adequately cover migrant workers employed primarily in construction and as domestic workers.

The government requires employers to declare their employees to the Ministry of Labor and to pay social security benefits. Penalties for noncompliance include a prison sentence of two to six months and a fine ranging from DZD 100,000 to DZD 200,000 ($916 to $1,832) and DZD 200,000 to DZD 500,000 ($1,832 to $4,579) for repeat offenders. In 2015 the director general of social security at the Ministry of Labor stated that employers had not declared 15 percent of workers to the government, down from 40 percent in 2001. Employers who violated the law faced DZD 200,000 ($1,832) fines and between two and six months in prison. An enforcement initiative in 2015 identified 13,473 undeclared workers, all but 3 percent of whom were employed in the private sector. The government allowed undeclared workers to gain credit for social security and retirement benefits for time spent in the informal economy if they repay any taxes owed after registering.

The Labor Ministry employed 624 labor inspectors and approximately 380 supervisors. The ministry generally enforced labor standards, including providing for compliance with the minimum wage regulation and safety standards. Nevertheless, broad enforcement remained insufficient.